Francis Creek Fjords Coloring Books: Color Your Way In
ISBN-13: 978-0-9971624-3-1
Copyright © 2016 Francis Creek Fjords, LLC, Francis Creek, WI. A...
Published by Francis Creek Fjords (www.FrancisCreekFjords.com). Printed by CreateSpace.

Patti Jo Walter and her husband, Dave Walter, started Francis Creek Fjords (FCF) in 1995. FCF was a Fjord hub for nearly two decades, having Fjords come from all over the United States to be trained, sold on consignment, or bred to their stallion, Fair Acres Ole. Patti Jo began giving riding lessons in 1998, teaching myriad disciplines: huntseat, dressage, jumping, and driving. Today, she continues to instruct dressage and jumping, sharing her passion with anyone wishing to learn and have fun with horses.

Patricia Holland, born and raised in Northeastern Pennsylvania, attended York Academy of Art to pursue a career in commercial art. Dovetailing her lifelong passions of art and horses, she became a professional horse trainer, illustrating what she saw, what she learned, and the people she met along the way. With humor and wit she juggles these contrasting careers, creating a rich and fulfilling life. She resides and illustrates in Galena, Illinois.

Norwegian Fjord Horses (N.F.H.), featured in many of these drawings, are an offshoot horse breed well known for their gentle disposition, calm demeanor, and great versatility, but it's their loving and humorous personalities that most owners are drawn to. Mutual affection for these charismatic animals caused Pat and Patti's lives to intersect. Once united, Pat's humor and wit served as the perfect complement to Patti's love of life, forging a lifelong friendship in and out of the pasture, much like the horses they admire.

Pat and Patti created this coloring book series as a fun way of learning horseback riding terminology and concepts for Francis Creek Fjords' students. Pat's skillfully drawn illustrations—filled with humor, life, and laughter—combined with Patti's impressive understanding of horses and students resulted in a colorful array of barnyard characters teaching valuable horse-related lessons you can color. Now we're doing Christmas ... with horses!

How to use this book

Step 1: Grab your crayons or colored pencils!
(Markers are not recommended)

· ·

Step 2: Choose your favorite picture!

· ·

Step 3: Color!

· ·

Step 4: Have fun!

· ·

Hopefully you enjoy this Christmas-themed coloring book as much as we enjoyed making it!

Horses are often associated with Christmas because many are good drivers, capable of dashing through the snow pulling an open sleigh!

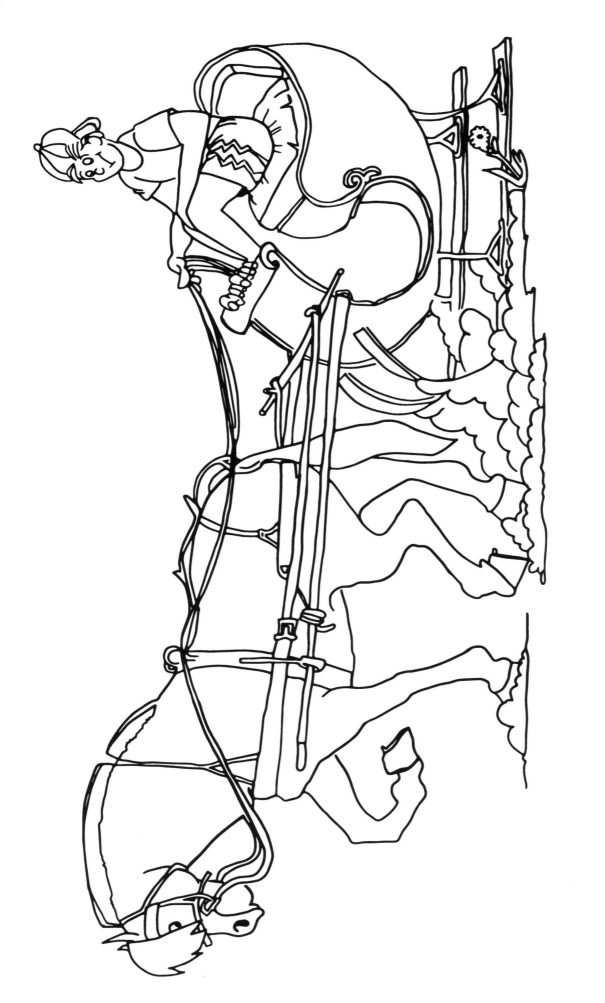

But horses won't dash through mud.
Sleighs need snow to glide on!

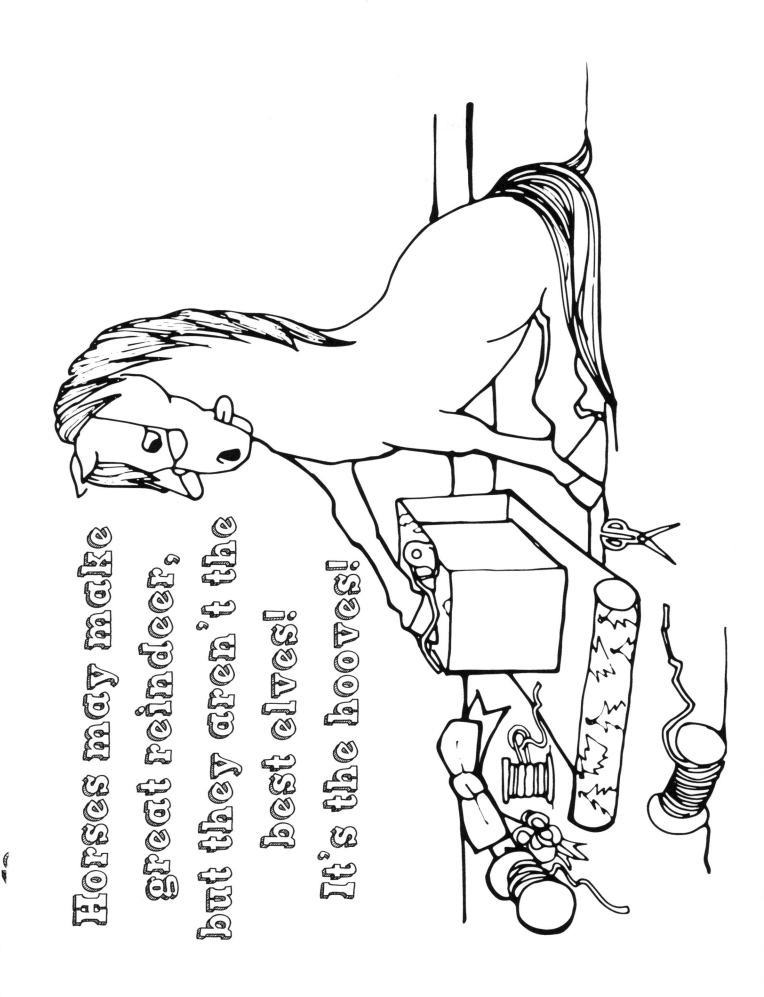

Horses may make
great reindeer,
but they aren't the
best elves!
It's the hooves!

And occasionally they lend Santa a helping hand!

And they can be very helpful friends!

Meet me by the mistletoe!

Wish for one, end up with four!

And then they grow up and want gifts
of their own!

I'd like some hay, and grain,
and peppermints, and carrots,
lots and lots of carrots!

I asked for carrots!

Don't forget to bundle up your horses. It gets cold out there!

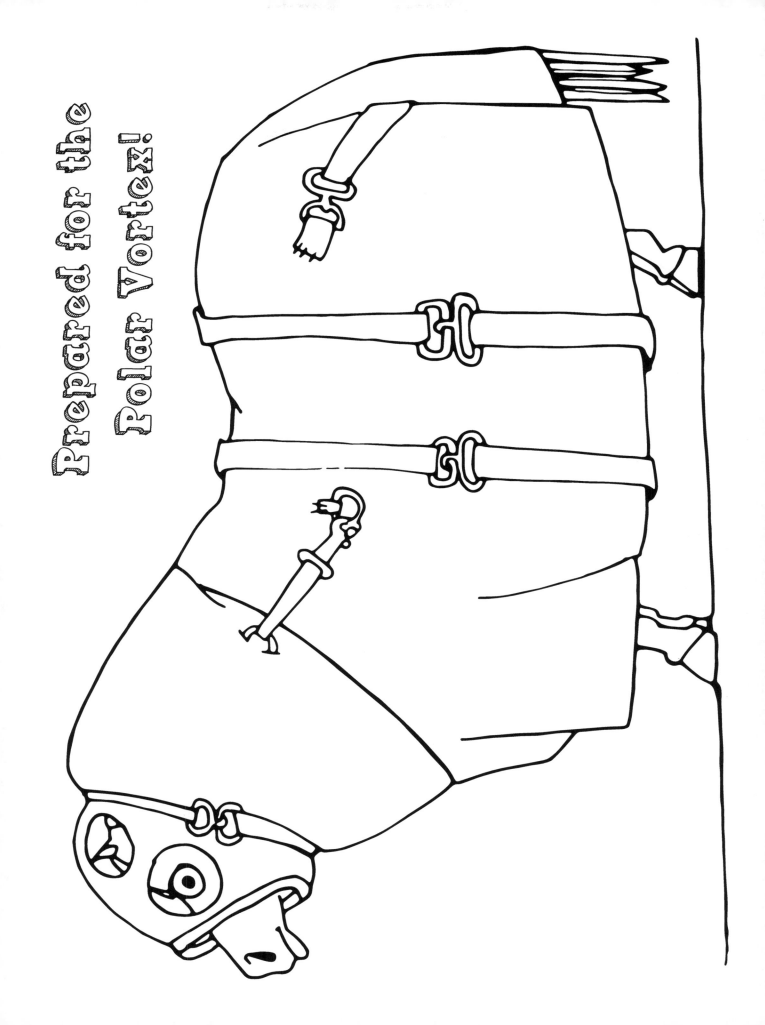

The best way to spread Christmas cheer is riding throughout the year!

Horses like to have fun in winter, too!
Build a snowman!

Catch snowflakes!

Go ice skating!

Fun Fjord Fact: Fjords are not primarily a driving horse!

We're always working on new books! Write to us (dwalter@tm.net) with your comments, ideas, or suggestions.

Francis Creek Fjords Coloring Books

Color Your Way Into
English Riding 1

By Patti Jo Walter and Pat Holland

You might also like:

Color Your Way Into English Riding 1!

Color Your Way Into English Riding 2!

Francis Creek Fjords Coloring Books

Color Your Way Into
English Riding 2

By Patti Jo Walter and Pat Holland

and ...

Color Your Way Into Western Riding!

Francis Creek Fjords Coloring **Books**

Color Your Way Into
Western Riding

By Patti Jo Walter and Pat Holland

Made in the USA
San Bernardino, CA
17 September 2016